GCSE AQA Combined Science

Chemistry

Required Practicals

Fire up the Bunsen burner — it's time to get to grips with those tricky GCSE Chemistry Required Practicals...

Luckily, this booklet has everything you need! It has heaps of write-in activities to develop your analysis and evaluation skills for all six Required Practicals. And there's plenty of exam-style practice too — you'll be an AQA practicals pro in no time.

To make sure you pick up every mark you can, we've included a mark-by-mark breakdown for every exam-style question. Plus, there are example answers for each task. You'll find those goodies in your **free** Online Edition — what a treat!

Unlock your Digital Extras

This booklet includes a **free Online Edition** including **full answers**. To access them, just scan the QR code below or go to **cgpbooks.co.uk/extras**, then enter this code!

Digital Extras

2278 2380 9067 5803

By the way, this code only works for one person. If somebody else has used this book before you, they might have already claimed the code.

Course Booklet
Higher Level

Published by CGP

From original material by Richard Parsons

Editors: Emma Clayton, Katherine Faudemer, Paul Jordin, Hannah Lawson

Contributors: Paddy Gannon, Jamie Sinclair, Jack Turner, Louise Watkins

With thanks to George Wright for the proofreading.
With thanks to Beth Linnane for the copyright research.

ISBN: 978 1 83774 189 2
Printed by Elanders Ltd, Newcastle upon Tyne.
Clipart from Corel®
Illustrations by: Sandy Gardner Artist, email sandy@sandygardner.co.uk

Contents

✓ Use the tick boxes to check off the pages you've completed.

Background Knowledge

In this practical, you'll be making **salt crystals** by reacting together an **acid** and a **base**.

Task 1 Circle the correct words in the definitions below.

ACID — a substance that forms aqueous solutions with a pH of **less than** / **greater than** 7.
BASE — a substance with a pH **less than** / **greater than** 7.
ALKALI — a base that dissolves in water to form a solution with a pH **less than** / **greater than** 7.

Task 2 Fill in the **ions** that make up the following salts.

Remember that the total charge of the negative ions must balance out the total charge of the positive ions.

KCl   NaNO₃   CuSO₄

Cl⁻

Task 3 Complete the equations for the following **neutralisation reactions**.

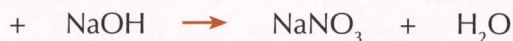

HCl + KOH ⟶ ☐ + H₂O

☐ + NaOH ⟶ NaNO₃ + H₂O

Key Definition
Neutralisation
A type of reaction between an acid and a base that produces neutral products.

Task 4 Jot down what you remember about **filtration** and **evaporation** to complete the mind maps. Think about what they are **used for** and what **equipment** is needed for each one.

e.g. used to separate insoluble solids from mixtures

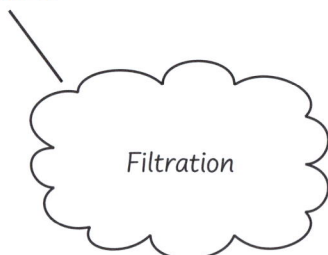

Filtration

Evaporation

Practical

Task 5 Use the **procedure** to help you answer the questions below.

Procedure

1 Set up a **Bunsen burner**, **tripod**, **gauze** and **heatproof mat** as shown in the diagram.

2 Add **40 cm³** of dilute **sulfuric acid** (H₂SO₄) to a **beaker**, and place it on the gauze.

3 Gently **heat** the acid. Turn off the Bunsen burner **just as** the acid starts to **boil**, and remove the beaker from the gauze.

4 Add a small amount of **copper(II) oxide** (**CuO**) powder to the acid. When stirred, the solution will turn **clear blue**.

5 **Repeat** step 4 until some copper(II) oxide **remains** after stirring.

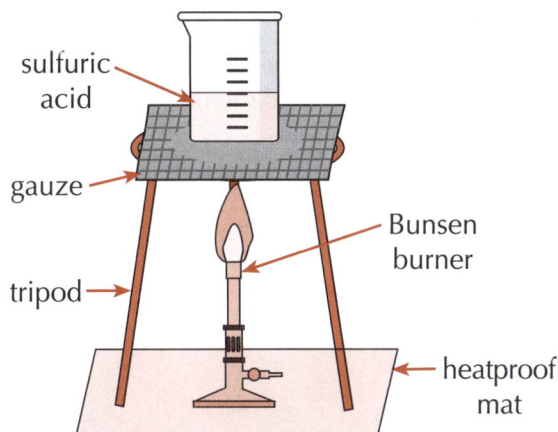

sulfuric acid

gauze

tripod

Bunsen burner

heatproof mat

If something is added in 'excess', more of it is added than will react.

Why is copper(II) oxide powder added to the sulfuric acid in **excess**?

....

....

Write a **balanced symbol equation** for the reaction between the acid and base in this procedure. Include **state symbols**.

+   ⟶   +

Task 6 Give three **safety precautions** that you should take when using the Bunsen burner to heat the acid in the procedure shown above.

1 ....

2 ....

3 ....

Neutralise the threat of poor practical technique...

DISCUSS

Why do you think dilute sulfuric acid is used in this procedure rather than concentrated sulfuric acid? Why is the acid removed from the heat just as it starts to boil? Discuss with a partner.

Practical

Task 7 **Draw** the filtration apparatus needed for the next step of the procedure.
Label the **salt solution**, **excess base**, **filter paper**, **funnel** and **conical flask**.

Procedure

6   Set up the **filter paper** and **filter funnel** over a **conical flask**.
    Filter the contents of the beaker into the flask.

Task 8   Use the **crystallisation** procedure below to help you label the diagram.

Procedure

7   Pour the contents of the conical
    flask into an **evaporating basin** and
    use a **water bath** to gently evaporate
    the water from the salt solution.

8   When **crystals** start to form, turn
    off the heat and pour the contents
    of the evaporating basin into a
    crystallising dish. Leave it to
    crystallise for a day or two.

9   Take the crystals out of the dish
    pat them dry using filter paper.

Key Definition

Water bath
*A container filled with heated water,
used to heat substances more
gently and evenly than direct heat.*

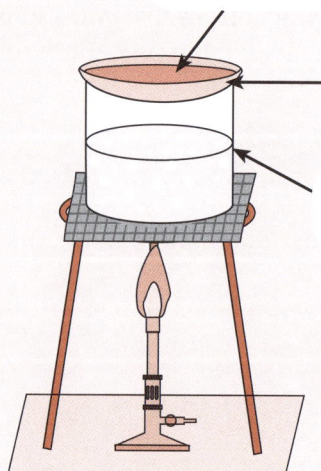

Evaluation

Task 9 The balanced equation for the reaction of **copper(II) oxide** with **hydrochloric acid** is:
$2HCl + CuO \rightarrow CuCl_2 + H_2O$

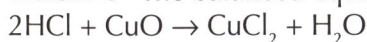

Samiyah says that by using **hydrochloric acid** instead of sulfuric acid, but keeping the volume and concentration of the acid the same, you will only need to add **half** the amount of copper(II) oxide. Is Samiyah correct? Explain your answer.

You can use the equation you wrote in Task 5 to help you with this.

....

....

....

....

Task 10 **Hydrated** copper(II) sulfate forms bright **blue crystals**. **Anhydrous** copper(II) sulfate is a **white powder**. This practical may produce blue crystals, a white powder, or a combination of both.

Two students carry out the procedure to produce pure copper(II) sulfate. India produces a **white powder** whereas Keiran produces **blue crystals**. Suggest what India might have done differently to Keiran.

....

....

Key Definitions
Hydrated salt
A salt that has water molecules present in its crystal structure.

Anhydrous salt
A salt containing no water molecules.

Task 11 The **yield** of a reaction is the mass of product made. Explain how each of the following changes to the procedure shown in tasks 5-8 would affect the yield of the experiment.

A student repeats the experiment but adds **half** the volume of **sulfuric acid**.

The student then repeats the experiment with the full volume of sulfuric acid but **half** the mass of **copper(II) oxide**.

DISCUSS

Anhydrous grapes in cookies — sneaky little blighters...
An electric water bath sets and maintains a constant, specified temperature. Discuss the pros and cons of using an electric water bath instead of a Bunsen burner in this experiment. Would it affect the results?

Exam-Style Questions

Task 12 Try these **exam-style** questions.

1   A student is trying to make pure calcium chloride crystals by reacting an acid
with an insoluble metal carbonate. They suggest the following method:

1. Add 40 cm³ of dilute sulfuric acid to a beaker.
2. Use a Bunsen burner to heat the beaker until the acid is hot,
then remove the beaker from the heat.
3. Add calcium carbonate powder to the beaker until some of it remains after stirring.
4. Pour the contents of the beaker into an evaporating basin and use a water bath to gently
heat the salt solution until all the water has evaporated.

1.1 This method will not produce pure calcium chloride crystals.
Explain why, and suggest how the method can be improved.

....

....

....

....

....

....

....

[3]

1.2 Zinc chloride is an ionic compound containing Zn^{2+} ions. The student attempts to make
zinc chloride crystals by adding an excess of insoluble zinc carbonate to hydrochloric acid.
Complete the balanced symbol equation for this reaction.

$$.....HCl + ... \rightarrow ZnCl_2 + H_2O + ...$$

[2]

1.3 When the reaction is complete, some zinc carbonate will remain after stirring.
Suggest another way that the student will know when the reaction is complete.

....

....

[1]

1.4 Sodium carbonate is soluble in water.
Another student suggests that to make sodium chloride, they could add sodium carbonate
to hydrochloric acid, then filter out the excess base and evaporate off the water.
Explain why this suggestion will not produce a pure sample of sodium chloride.

....

....

[1]

[Total 8 marks]

Background Knowledge

In this practical, we'll investigate what happens when two different **aqueous solutions** are **electrolysed**.

Task 1 Add the metals in the box to the **reactivity series**, listing them in order from **most** reactive at the top to **least** reactive at the bottom.

Hint: the metals that are less reactive than hydrogen are ones you might find in jewellery.

Reactivity Series

....

....

Carbon

....

....

Hydrogen

....

....

Magnesium   Zinc

Sodium

Silver

Iron   Copper

Task 2 **Draw lines** to match the words to their definitions.

| Oxidation | Reduction | Cation | Anion |

Positive ion   Gain of electrons   Negative ion   Loss of electrons

Task 3 **Ionic equations** show only the particles that **react** and the products they form.

For the following ionic equation, circle the reactant that is being **reduced**.

$$Mg + Cu^{2+} \longrightarrow Mg^{2+} + Cu$$

Explain how you know this.

Background Knowledge

Task 4 For each of the following **half equations**, decide whether they would take place at the **anode** (positive electrode) or **cathode** (negative electrode) during electrolysis.

	Anode	Cathode
$Al^{3+} + 3e^- \rightarrow Al$	☐	☐
$2H^+ + 2e^- \rightarrow H_2$	☐	☐
$2O^{2-} \rightarrow O_2 + 4e^-$	☐	☐
$2Br^- \rightarrow Br_2 + 2e^-$	☐	☐

Key Definitions

Half equation
An equation showing either the reduction or oxidation part of a redox reaction, in terms of the movement of electrons.

Redox reaction
A reaction that involves the transfer of electrons.

Task 5 **Electrolysis** can be performed on **molten ionic compounds** and **aqueous solutions**. Give all the **ions** present in the following:

> **Molten magnesium oxide**

> **Aqueous potassium iodide**

Task 6 Fill in the gaps in the flow chart to show what **products** are made at each electrode during the electrolysis of an **aqueous solution** of a **metal salt**.

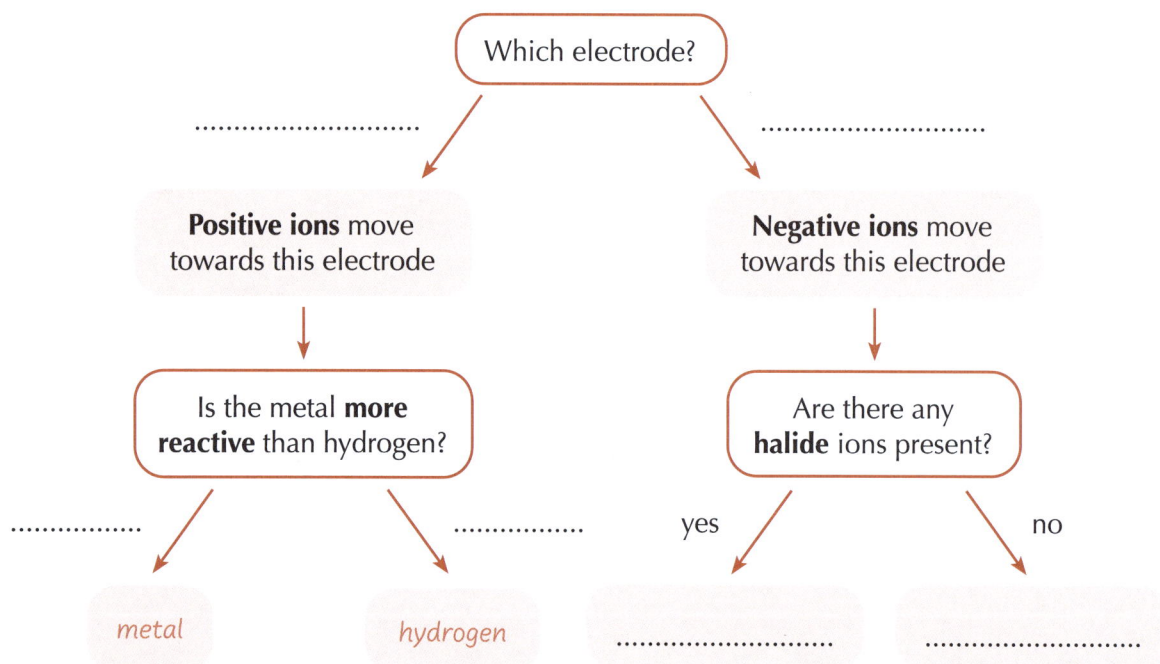

Which electrode?

....

Positive ions move towards this electrode

Negative ions move towards this electrode

Is the metal **more reactive** than hydrogen?

Are there any **halide** ions present?

....   yes   no

metal   *hydrogen*   ....

DISCUSS

Never trust iodide — I can't tell you all the times halide...

You need to be able to write half equations for the reactions that happen at the electrodes. Are there any patterns that you can use to work out unknown half equations? Discuss with a partner.

Practical

Task 7   In this practical, we'll be electrolysing **copper(II) chloride** solution and **sodium chloride** solution. Write a **hypothesis** for what you expect to be produced at each electrode when these solutions are electrolysed.

You'll need to give the states as well as the names of the products.

Copper(II) chloride solution

.... will be

produced at the anode.

.... will be

produced at the cathode.

Sodium chloride solution

Key Definition

Hypothesis
*A statement of what
you expect to happen
in an experiment —
it can be accepted
or rejected.*

Task 8   The procedure for setting up an **electrochemical cell** is given below.
Draw a diagram of the set up, labelling the **electrolyte solution**, **anode** and **cathode**.

Procedure

1   Pour the **electrolyte solution** into a **beaker**.
2   Add a **lid**, e.g. a piece of cardboard with two holes in it. Poke the **electrodes** through the holes.
3   Use crocodile leads to connect the electrodes to a **low-voltage power supply**.
4   **Turn on** the power supply.
5   **Observe** and **record** what happens at each electrode.

d.c. power supply

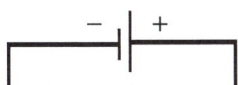

− | +

Key Definitions

Electrolyte
*A liquid or solution that can
conduct electricity.*

Electrode
*A solid that conducts
electricity and is submerged
in the electrolyte.*

Practical

Task 9 You can use inert **carbon rods** as electrodes in this practical.

Why is it important that the electrodes are **inert**?

....

You must make sure that the electrodes **aren't touching** when
you set up your electrochemical cell. Suggest why.

....

....

Why should you **rinse** your electrodes and beaker with **distilled water** between solutions?

....

....

Task 10 For each of the following elements, suggest what you would **observe**
if it was formed during electrolysis, and how you could **test** for its presence.
Think about the **state** you would expect to find the element in.

Chlorine

Hydrogen

Oxygen

Mitochondria are the powerhouses... Sorry, wrong cell...
Different halogens have different states at room temperature. Discuss with a partner what you
would expect to observe if fluorine, bromine or iodine were produced at an electrode.

Results, Analysis and Conclusions

Task 11 The table below shows some **example results** from this practical.
For each observation, state which **element** was produced.

Solution	Anode (positive electrode)		Cathode (negative electrode)	
	Observations	Element produced	Observations	Element produced
Copper(II) chloride	Bubbles Turns damp litmus paper white		Red/brown coating on electrode	
Sodium chloride	Bubbles Turns damp litmus paper white		Rapid bubbles	

Task 12 Do the example results in the table above line up with your hypotheses from **Task 7**?
Circle whether your hypotheses would be **accepted** or **rejected** and explain why.

Copper(II) chloride solution	Sodium chloride solution
Anode: I **accept / reject** my hypothesis. Explanation: I hypothesised that .... would be produced at the anode. .... was produced.	**Anode:** I **accept / reject** my hypothesis. Explanation:
Cathode: I **accept / reject** my hypothesis. Explanation:	**Cathode:** I **accept / reject** my hypothesis. Explanation:

DISCUSS

I accept / reject my hypothesis that chemistry is boring...

Testing hypotheses is the backbone of how science works. Discuss what you think makes a good hypothesis. Can you think of anything else you'd like to find out based on your results from this practical?

Results, Analysis and Conclusions

Task 13 Write the balanced **half equations** for the reactions that occurred at each electrode.

Think about what's being produced and whether electrons are being gained or lost.

Copper(II) chloride (CuCl$_2$)

Anode $\longrightarrow$ +

Cathode   + $\longrightarrow$

Sodium chloride (NaCl)

Anode $\longrightarrow$ +

Cathode   + $\longrightarrow$

Task 14 A student electrolysed **copper(II) sulfate solution**, weighing the cathode every five minutes. The graph below shows the change in mass of the cathode over time.

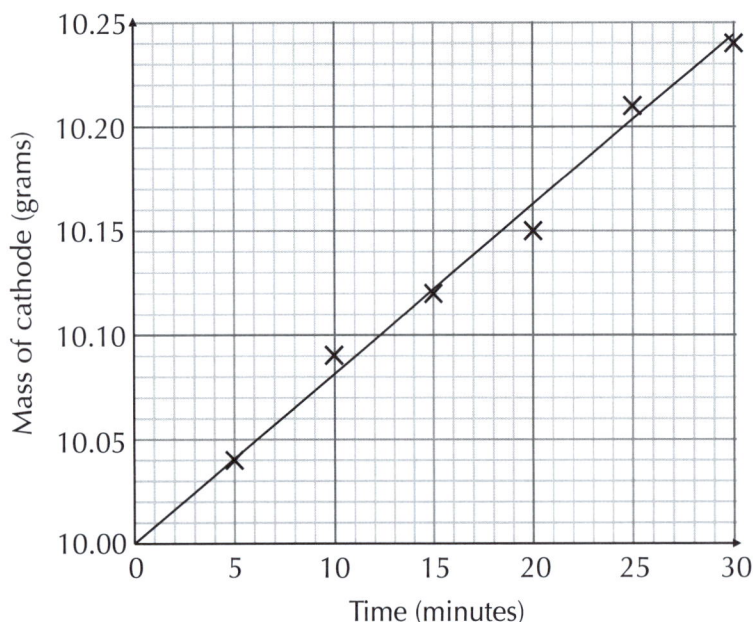

What is the mass of the cathode after **16 minutes**?

.... g

Describe and explain how the mass of the cathode **changed** over time.

....

....

....

Exam-Style Questions

Task 15 Try these **exam-style** questions.

1 Some students investigated the electrolysis of aqueous silver nitrate solution.
Silver nitrate solution contains Ag^+ and NO_3^- ions.
The diagram below shows the apparatus the students used.

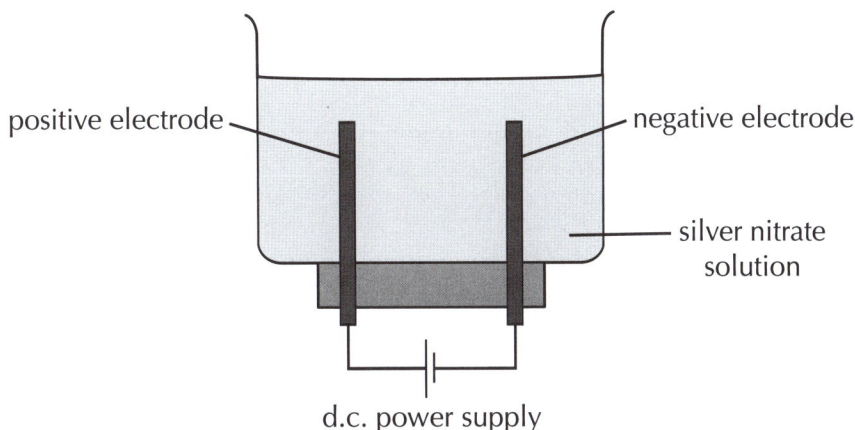

positive electrode — negative electrode — silver nitrate solution — d.c. power supply

After five minutes, a coating of silver could be seen on the negative electrode.

1.1 Explain why silver ions move towards the negative electrode.

....
[1]

1.2 Complete the balanced half equation for the reaction at the negative electrode.

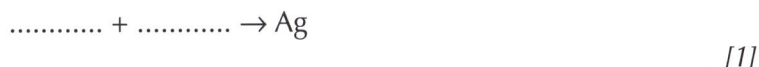

$$............. + ... \rightarrow Ag$$

[1]

1.3 A gas is produced at the positive electrode. Name the gas and describe how it is formed.

....
....
[2]

1.4 Complete the balanced half equation for the reaction at the positive electrode.

$$4OH^- \rightarrow .... + ... + ...$$

[1]

1.5 The students want to find out how the volume of gas produced changes over time.
Outline how they could investigate this.

....
....
....
....
[4]

[Total 9 marks]

Background Knowledge

In this practical we're investigating **temperature changes**. Most reactions involve some sort of change in temperature, so there are lots of ways to study how different **variables** affect temperature change.

Task 1   The heat energy in some chemical reactions is transferred from the reaction mixture to the surroundings. Suggest **two** ways to **reduce** this energy transfer when you are conducting an experiment.

....

....

....

Task 2   **Lines of best fit** can be drawn as straight lines or smooth curves.
Two copies of the same graph are shown below, with part of a line of best fit added.

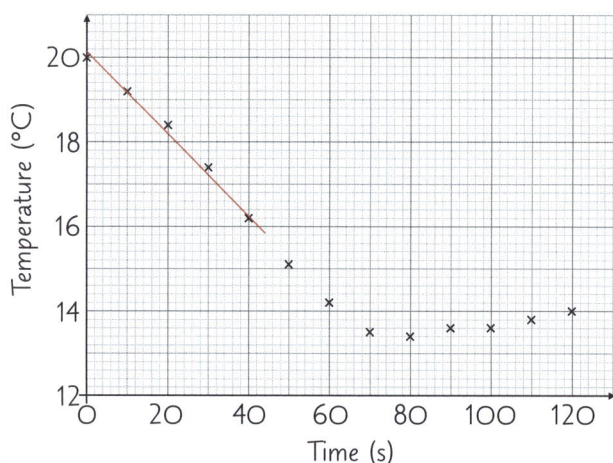

1   Use the line of best fit to estimate the temperature at a time of **38 seconds**.
Give your answer to 3 significant figures.

°C

2   On the first graph, extend the straight line of best fit and add a second straight line through the rest of the data points.

Key Definition
Line of best fit
A straight line or curve on a scatter graph, drawn through or close to as many points as possible.

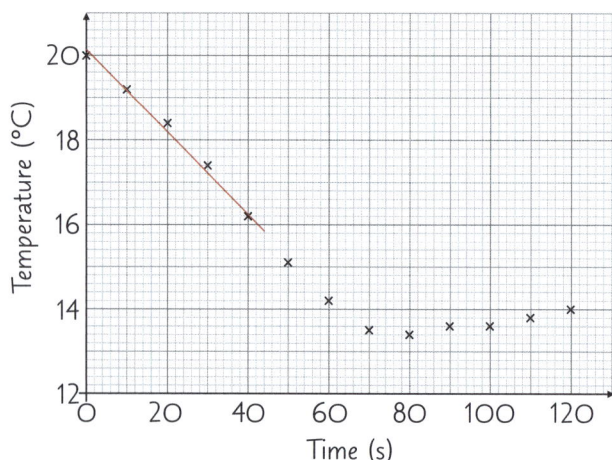

3   On the second graph, extend the existing line of best fit to make a smooth curve that passes as close as possible to the data points.

4   Use your curved line of best fit to estimate when the **minimum temperature** was reached.
Give your answer to the nearest second.

seconds

Lines of best fit can be curved or straight. Always check if the instructions for a task or question specify one or the other, and make sure you draw the right sort.

Hope that's got you warmed up...

DISCUSS

With a partner, see if you can think of any reactions that result in a change in temperature. Do any of them have anything in common? What would you need to accurately measure the temperature?

Practical

Task 3 The reaction between hydrochloric acid and sodium hydroxide solution results in an **increase** in temperature. An experiment to investigate how changing the **volume** of sodium hydroxide solution affects the **temperature change** in this reaction is outlined below.

Procedure

Add 30 cm³ of dilute hydrochloric acid to a polystyrene cup, then measure the temperature of the acid.

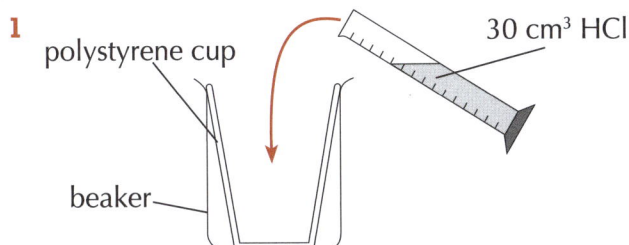

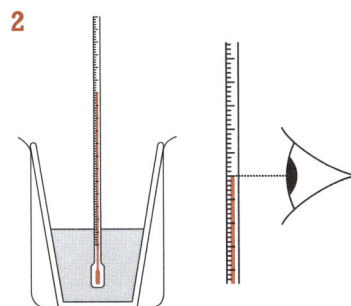

1
polystyrene cup
30 cm³ HCl
beaker

2

Add 5 cm³ of dilute sodium hydroxide solution to the acid, then quickly fit a lid to the cup. Use the thermometer to stir the mixture. Record the highest temperature the mixture reaches.

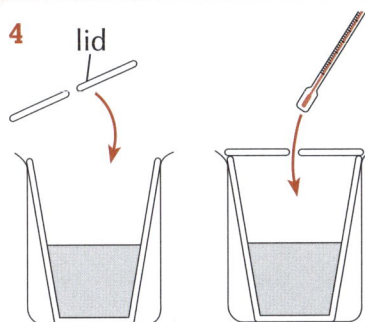

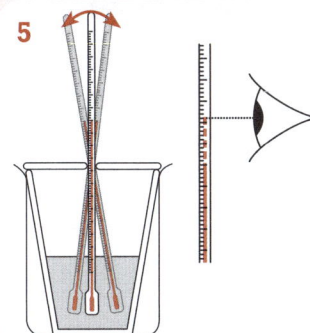

3 5 cm³ NaOH solution

4 lid

5

Carry on adding sodium hydroxide solution, 5 cm³ at a time. Record the maximum temperature reached each time. Keep going until you've added a total of 40 cm³ of sodium hydroxide solution.

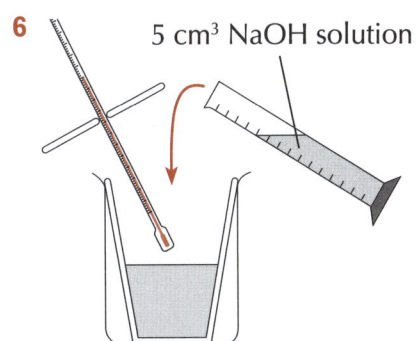

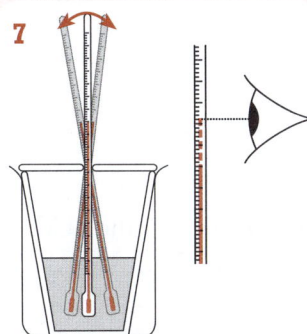

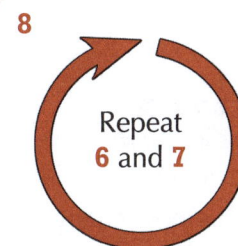

6 5 cm³ NaOH solution

7

8 Repeat **6** and **7**

Both reactants in this experiment are **corrosive**. What **safety precautions** should you take when working with the corrosive chemicals used here?

....

....

....

Practical

Task 4 **Neutralisation reactions** between acids and alkalis release energy which heats the surroundings. Add more **variables** to the mind map that could affect the **temperature change** in a neutralisation reaction.

Key Definition

Neutralisation
A reaction between an acid and a base that produces neutral products.

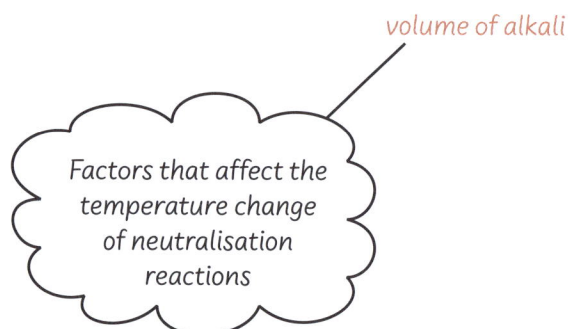

volume of alkali

Factors that affect the temperature change of neutralisation reactions

Task 5 Two more reactions which result in an increase in temperature are given below. For each one, briefly **describe** how you could **adapt** the procedure given in **Task 3** to carry out the given investigation.

Acid Plus Carbonate

Hydrochloric acid reacts with copper carbonate: $2HCl_{(aq)} + CuCO_{3(s)} \rightarrow CuCl_{2(aq)} + CO_{2(g)} + H_2O_{(l)}$
Investigate how changing the **mass** of **copper carbonate** affects the temperature change in this reaction.

Acid Plus Metal

Sulfuric acid reacts with magnesium: $H_2SO_{4(aq)} + Mg_{(s)} \rightarrow MgSO_{4(aq)} + H_{2(g)}$
Investigate how changing the **concentration** of the **acid** affects the temperature change in this reaction.

DISCUSS

Keep a lid on it... except when you have to take the lid off to add more reactant...

All the reactions covered on these pages involve an increase in temperature. Discuss whether you would need to change the method for a reaction where the temperature decreased instead. Why, or why not?

Results, Analysis and Conclusions

Task 6 Keira carried out the experiment described in Task 3. Her **results** are shown below. **Complete** the table by working out the **mean value** for the maximum temperature reached for each volume of sodium hydroxide solution.

Give your answers to **3 significant figures**. The first one has been done for you.

Volume of NaOH solution added (cm³)	Maximum temperature (°C) — Trial 1	Maximum temperature (°C) — Trial 2	Mean maximum temperature (°C)
0	19.8	20.5	20.2
5	23.5	23.9	
10	26.0	25.8	
15	28.8	28.2	
20	31.0	30.5	
25	32.1	32.4	
30	32.3	32.4	
35	32.1	31.5	
40	30.5	31.0	

Task 7 Using the data from the table above, plot a graph on this grid to show the relationship between the volume of NaOH solution and temperature. Use the **mean temperature values** you calculated and choose a **sensible scale** for each axis.

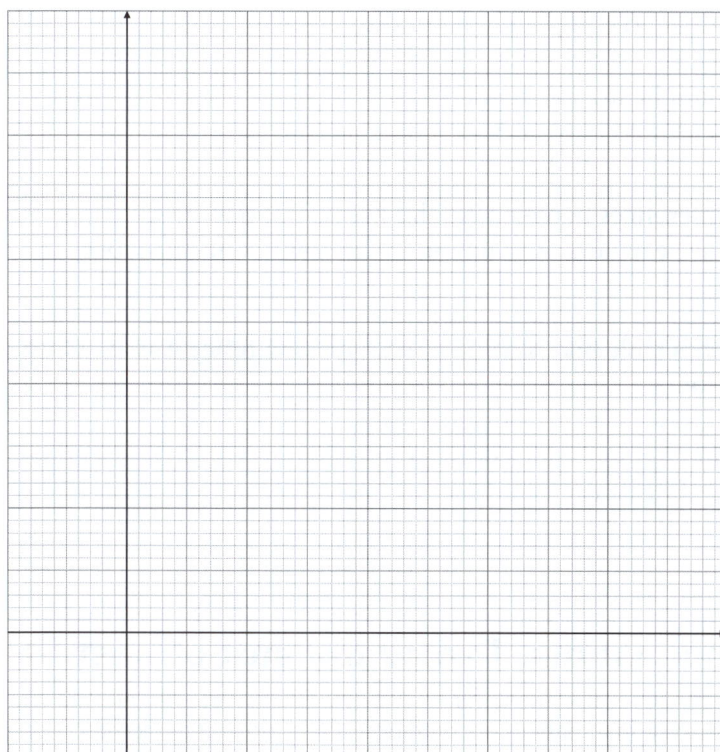

Remember to put the independent variable on the x-axis and the dependent variable on the y-axis.

Key Definitions

Dependent variable
The variable that you measure when you're doing an experiment.

Independent variable
The variable that you change when you're doing an experiment.

Results, Analysis and Conclusions

Task 8 Noah carried out **his own version** of the experiment. The graph below shows Noah's data.

Draw two **straight lines of best fit** on Noah's graph, extending them so that they cross.

Mean maximum temperature (°C)

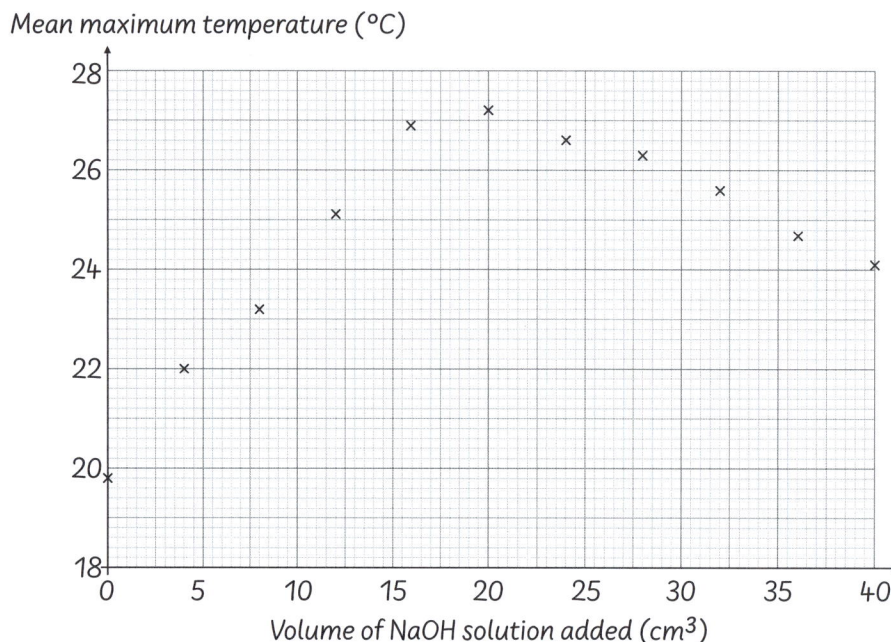

Volume of NaOH solution added (cm³)

Task 9 The maximum temperature reached in this reaction can be **estimated** using the lines of best fit.

> Calculate the temperature change that occurred in this reaction.
>
> .... °C

The maximum temperature is reached at the point where enough sodium hydroxide has been added to **completely neutralise** the acid.

> Estimate the volume of sodium hydroxide needed to
> completely neutralise the acid used in Noah's experiment: ....cm³

Task 10 There were some **differences** between Noah's method and Keira's.
For example, Noah used the **same reactants** as Keira but in **different concentrations**.

> Using information from Keira's table and Noah's graph, give **one other way** in which Noah's
> method was different from Keira's.
>
> ....
>
> ....

DISCUSS

On special occasions, I wear my suit of best fit...

With a partner, compare the results shown for Keira's and Noah's experiments. In which experiment do
you think the reactants were in a higher concentration? Why do you think that? Can you tell for sure?

Evaluation

Task 11 The procedure given in Task 3 will **not** always give an **accurate** value
for the temperature change in the reaction.

Looking in particular at the method used in **steps 6-8** of the procedure, suggest one reason why
the true temperature change is likely to be **higher** than the values recorded in this experiment.

....

....

Explain how this might affect the **reproducibility** of the results.

....

....

....

....

Key Definition

Reproducibility
*How easy it is for
different people to
get similar results
when carrying out
the same experiment.*

Suggest **two changes** to this experiment that would improve the **accuracy** of the data recorded.

1	2

Task 12 When a line of best fit is **extended** and used to estimate values
outside the range of the data points, this is called **extrapolation**.

Hint: think about what the graph would look
like if you only had the first few data values
for one of the experiments in this practical.

Explain, using temperature change investigations as an example,
why you might get **misleading** estimates if you extrapolate beyond the range of your data.

....

....

....

....

....

DISCUSS For reproducible results, stick 'em in the photocopier...
Are there any other steps in this method that might affect the accuracy of your results, apart from any
you've mentioned above? Discuss with a partner any other potential sources of error in this experiment.

Exam-Style Questions

Task 13 Try these exam-style questions.

1   Copper can be displaced from a solution of copper chloride by adding a more reactive metal. For example, the reaction between copper chloride and zinc is:

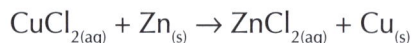

$$CuCl_{2(aq)} + Zn_{(s)} \rightarrow ZnCl_{2(aq)} + Cu_{(s)}$$

This type of reaction is exothermic. A student is designing an investigation into how the temperature change is affected by changing which metal is added.

1.1 The metals that the student is considering comparing are sodium, calcium, magnesium, zinc, iron and tin. Using your knowledge of the reactivity of metals, suggest why using sodium and calcium would not give a fair comparison with the other metals on this list.

   ....

   ....

   [1]

The experiment will involve a series of tests. In each test, the student will add a sample of a different metal to a test tube containing copper chloride solution. The same volume and concentration of copper chloride solution will be used in each test.

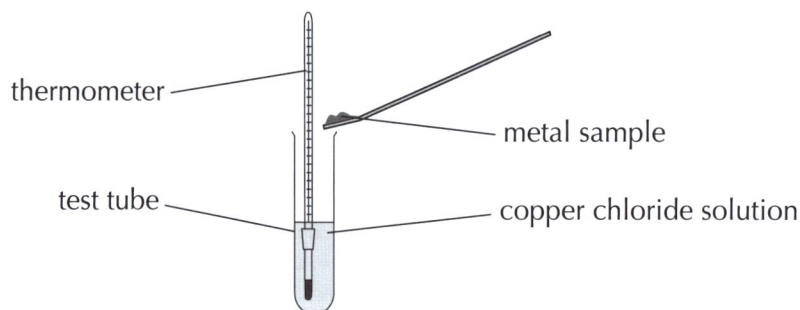

thermometer — | — metal sample

test tube — | — copper chloride solution

1.2 Which reactant should be in excess in each test, the metal or the copper chloride solution? Explain your answer.

   ....

   ....

   ....

   [2]

1.3 The student says, "In each test, I will record the temperature of the reaction mixture every 15 seconds for 2 minutes." Explain how this part of the method could be improved.

   ....

   ....

   ....

   [2]

   [Total 5 marks]

Practical 11: Rates of Reaction

Background Knowledge

Here we'll be investigating how changes in **concentration** affect the **rates of reactions**. You'll be treated to two experiments — one involving **measuring gases** and the other looking at **turbidity** changes. Yippee.

Task 1 The graph below shows the **rate** of a reaction taking place under three **different conditions**.

The y axis could also show the amount of reactant used.

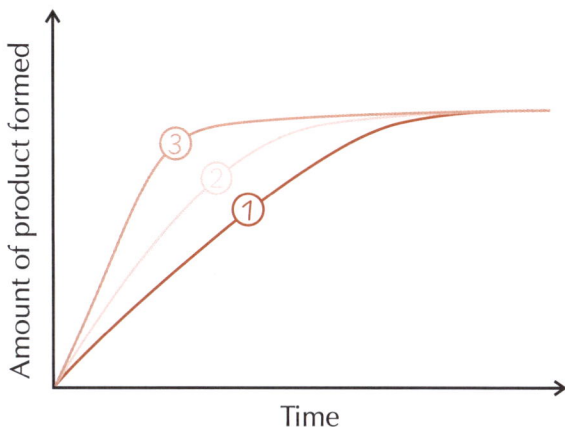

Amount of product formed

③ ② ①

Time

Key Definition
Rate of reaction
The speed at which the reactants are changed into products.

Under which set of conditions was the reaction **fastest**?

1   2   3

☐   ☐   ☐

Task 2 Make notes on the factors that influence the rate of a reaction. Think about **how** and **why** they affect the rate, referring to **collision theory** and whether the **state** of the reactants matters. You may find it helpful to include **diagrams** in your notes. The first one has been done for you.

Concentration / Pressure

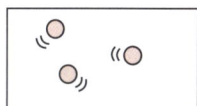

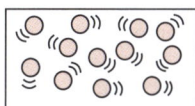

Low conc. / pressure   High conc. / pressure

Increase in concentration or pressure increases rate as more particles in same volume, so more frequent collisions. Concentration affects solutions, pressure affects gases.

Temperature

Adding a catalyst can also speed up a reaction by lowering the activation energy (the energy needed for the reaction to occur).

Surface Area

Background Knowledge

Task 3 Draw **lines of best fit** on the graphs below.
They should be **smooth curves** that come close to all the points.

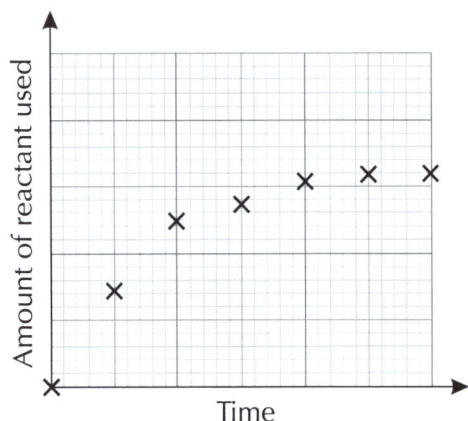

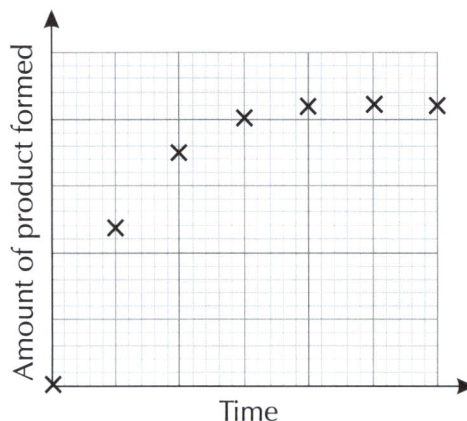

Task 4 The graph below shows the **volume of gas** released by a reaction over **time**.

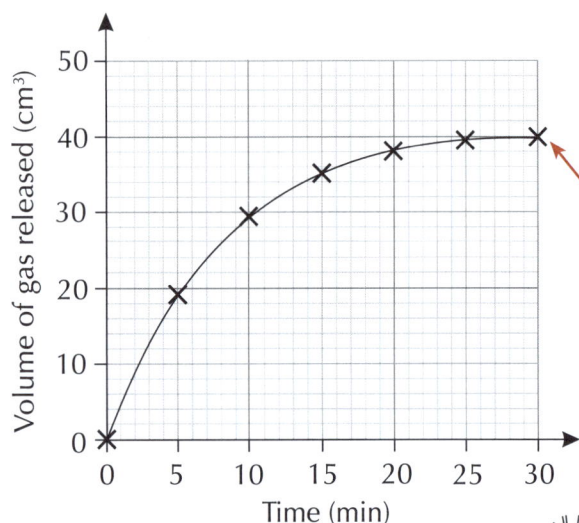

Complete this calculation to find the **mean** rate of the reaction during the time shown on the graph.
Give your answer to **2 significant figures**.

$$Rate\ of\ reaction = \frac{Amount\ of\ product\ formed}{Time}$$

The total amount of gas released (product formed)

was .... cm^3.

The time taken was .... minutes.

Mean rate of reaction = ... ÷ .... = ...

.... cm^3/min

You can also find the rate using the amount of reactant used instead of the amount of product formed, depending on what you measure in your experiment.

What is the rate of the reaction at **10 minutes**?
Give your answer to **2 significant figures**.

1. Draw a tangent on the graph
2. Find the coordinates of two points on the tangent
3. Use the formula below to calculate the gradient:

   gradient = change in y ÷ change in x

Key Definition
Tangent
A straight line that touches a curve at a point without crossing it.

.... cm^3/min

🅓 **I'm working at a mean rate of 4.6 p/h (puns per hour)...**
Think about some real life chemical reactions, e.g. combustion (burning), rusting, photosynthesis (how plants make glucose). Discuss whether they are fast or slow, and why you think that is.

Practical — Activity 1

Task 5 This activity involves measuring the rate of reaction between **magnesium** and **hydrochloric acid**. The **concentration** of the acid will be changed, but all other variables will stay the same.

A hypothesis is a statement of what you expect to happen in an experiment — it can be accepted or rejected.

Write a **hypothesis** stating how you expect the **concentration** of hydrochloric acid to affect the **rate** of this reaction.

Use **collision theory** to explain your hypothesis.

Task 6 Use the **procedure** to answer the question below.

Key Definition
Delivery tube
A thin glass tube used to allow gas to travel from one container to another.

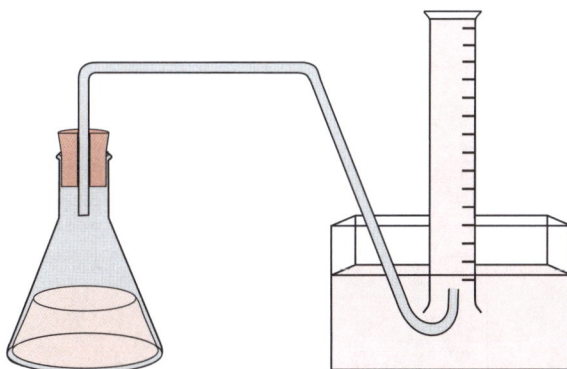

Procedure

1   Add **50 cm³** of **1.0 mol/dm³** hydrochloric acid to a **conical flask**.
2   Set up the **conical flask** with a **bung, delivery tube**, **water trough** and **measuring cylinder** as shown in the diagram. Make sure the upturned measuring cylinder is **completely filled** with water.
3   Remove the bung from the flask and add a **3 cm** strip of **magnesium ribbon** to the acid.
4   Quickly put the bung back on the flask and start a **stopwatch**.
5   Every **10 seconds**, check the measuring cylinder and record the **volume** of hydrogen gas. Continue until the volume **stops increasing**.
6   Now **repeat** the experiment using the same volume of **1.5 mol/dm³** hydrochloric acid.

Measurements of the volume of gas produced must be taken **every 10 seconds**.
Describe how you can work with your partner to ensure the measurements are made **accurately**.

....

....

....

....

Results and Analysis

Task 7 The table below shows some **example results** from this experiment. **Plot** both sets of data on the graph paper below and draw a **line of best fit** for each. **Label** each line with the acid concentration.

Time (seconds)		10	20	30	40	50	60	70	80	90
Volume of gas produced (cm³)	1.0 mol/ dm³	7.0	15.0	20.0	29.0	34.0	41.0	45.0	49.0	49.0
	1.5 mol/ dm³	11.0	21.0	33.0	43.0	50.0	54.0	55.0	55.0	55.0

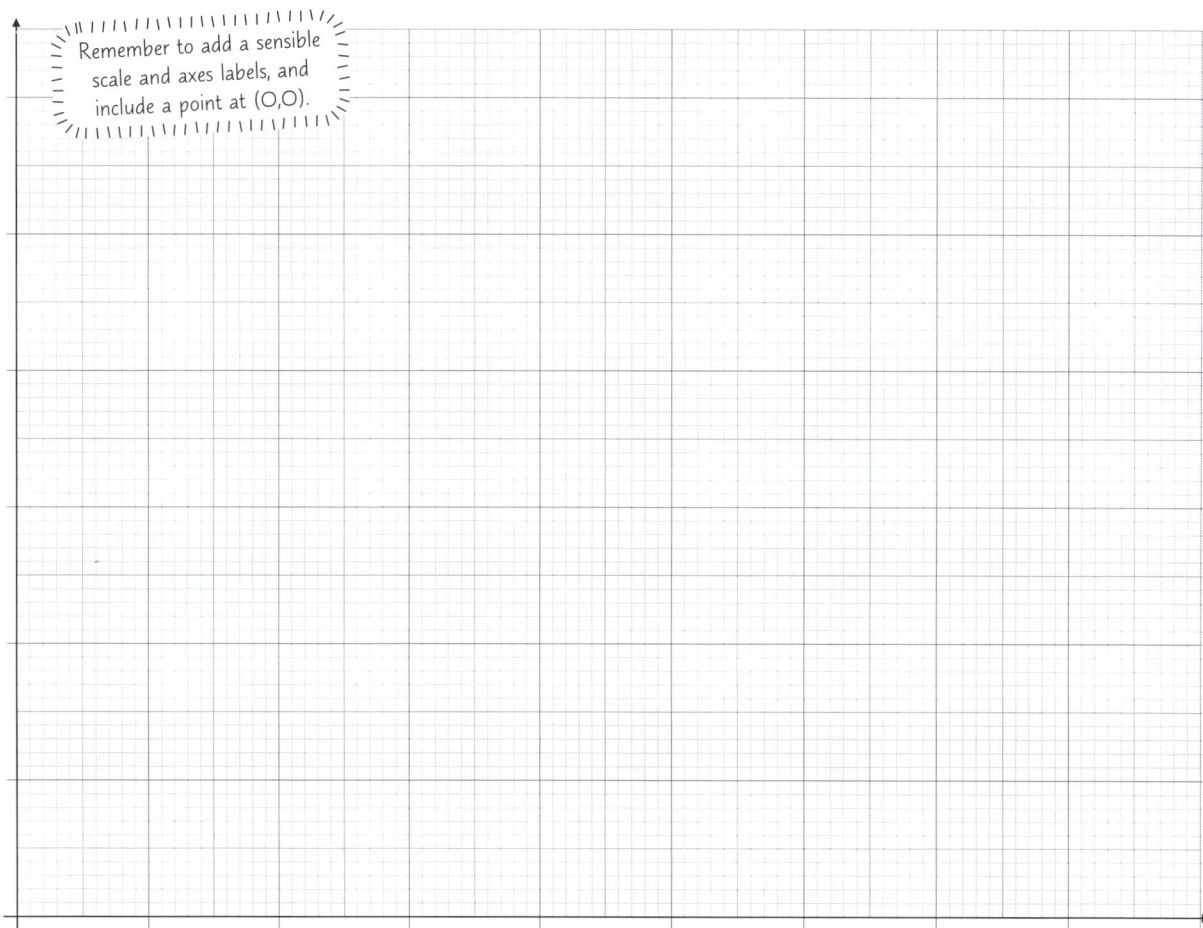

Remember to add a sensible scale and axes labels, and include a point at (0,0).

Task 8 Based on the example results, state whether you would accept or reject your hypothesis from **Task 5**. Use the **graph** to explain your answer.

DISCUSS

Higher concentration of beans = more gas production...

What products are formed in this reaction? Discuss with a partner, using your knowledge of how metals react with acids. You can even have a go at writing a balanced symbol equation.

Conclusions and Evaluation

Task 9 Calculate the **mean rate** of reaction until the reaction **finished** (when no more gas was produced) for both concentrations of acid. Give your answers to **two significant figures**.

There's a formula for this on page 22.

1.0 mol/dm³:

.... cm³/s

1.5 mol/dm³:

.... cm³/s

Task 10 Calculate the rate of reaction at **60 seconds** for both concentrations of acid. Draw a **tangent** on the graph for each concentration and find the **gradient** of the lines. Give your answers to **two significant figures**.

1.0 mol/dm³:

.... cm³/s

1.5 mol/dm³:

.... cm³/s

Task 11 How do the rates you calculated in **Task 9** compare to the rates you calculated in **Task 10**? Use **collision theory** to explain why they're different.

....

....

....

....

....

....

....

Conclusions and Evaluation

Task 12 A student repeats the experiment but uses a **gas syringe** instead of a water trough and measuring cylinder, as shown in the diagram below.

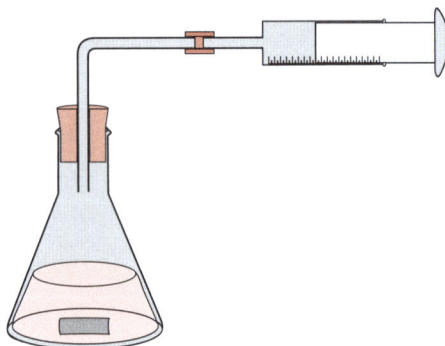

Key Definition

Gas syringe
A syringe used to insert, withdraw or measure gas.

The student tests **three** different concentrations of hydrochloric acid:
1.0 mol/dm³, **1.5 mol/dm³** and **2.0 mol/dm³**.

Give one **advantage** of using a gas syringe instead of a water trough and measuring cylinder.

....

....

How would you expect the rate of reaction with **2.0 mol/dm³** hydrochloric
acid to compare to the rate with **1.5 mol/dm³** hydrochloric acid?

....

The student measures a **larger overall volume** of gas when using **1.5 mol/dm³**
hydrochloric acid compared to **1.0 mol/dm³**. Explain why.

....

....

....

The student **does not** measure a larger overall volume of gas when using **2.0 mol/dm³**
hydrochloric acid compared to **1.5 mol/dm³**. Suggest why.

....

The student says that using the same mass of **powdered** magnesium would
increase the rate of the reaction. Are they correct? Explain your answer.

....

....

....

DISCUSS

If it's a gas syringe, how do you pick it up...?

Discuss what you'd expect to see if you measured the mass of the open conical flask and its contents instead of collecting the gas. How would the change in mass compare to the volume of gas produced?

Practical — Activity 2

Task 13 This next activity involves observing changes in the **turbidity** (cloudiness) of a solution.
Fill in the missing **volumes** in the table below.

Procedure

1. Add 50 cm³ of 40 g/dm³ **sodium thiosulfate** solution to a **conical flask**.
2. Put the conical flask on a **piece of paper** with a **black cross** printed on it.
3. Add **10 cm³** of dilute **hydrochloric acid** to the conical flask while gently swirling the flask. Start a **stopwatch**.
4. Look down at the cross through the flask. When you can no longer see the cross, **stop** the stopwatch and **record** the time taken for the cross to disappear.
5. **Repeat** steps 1-4 another four times. For each repeat, mix the **original 40 g/dm³ solution** with **water** in different proportions, as shown in the table below.
   This will give a different **concentration** of sodium thiosulfate solution each time.
   The **total volume** of solution used, including the water, should be **the same** for each repeat.

Volume of sodium thiosulfate (cm³)	Volume of water (cm³)	Concentration of sodium thiosulfate solution (g/dm³)
50		40
	10	32
		24
	30	16
10	40	8

Task 14 Give the **independent** variable, **dependent** variable and two **control** variables for this experiment.

Independent variable:

Dependent variable:

Control variables:

Key Definitions
Independent variable
The variable you change.

Dependent variable
The variable you measure.

Control variable
A variable you keep the same.

X marks the spot... X marks the spot... X marks the spot...

DISCUSS

For each of the control variables you gave in Task 14, discuss why you think it's important that the variable is kept the same throughout the experiment. Can you think of any more control variables?

Results and Analysis

Task 15 The table below shows some **example results** from the experiment.
Calculate the **mean** time taken for the cross to disappear for the different concentrations.
Give your answers to **the nearest second**.

Concentration of sodium thiosulfate solution (g/dm³)	Time taken for cross to disappear (seconds)			
	First trial	Second trial	Third trial	Mean
8	140	139	138	
16	74	76	74	
24	49	46	45	
32	40	37	36	
40	25	24	26	

Task 16 **Plot** the **concentration** of sodium thiosulfate solution against the **mean time** taken for the cross to disappear on the graph paper below. Draw a **line of best fit**.

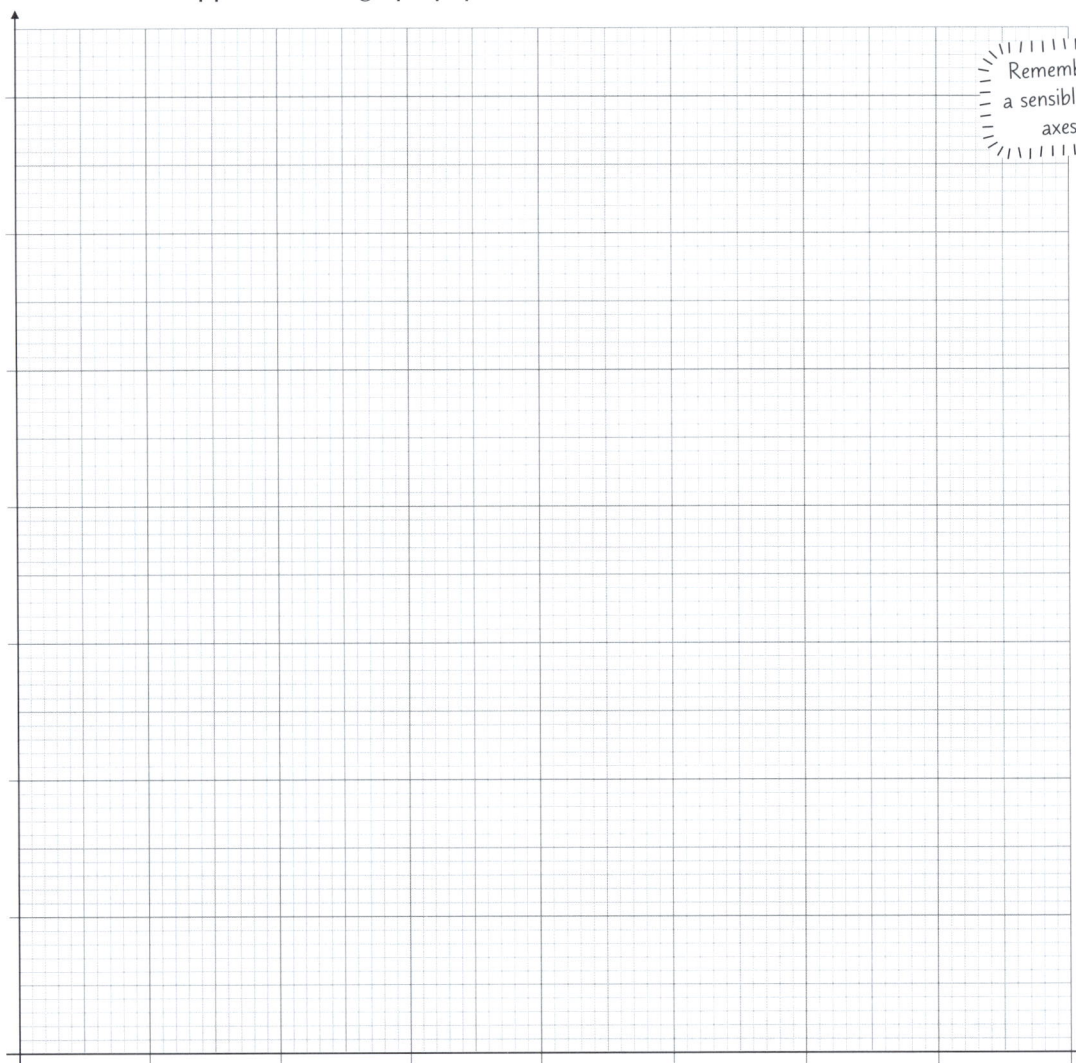

Remember to add a sensible scale and axes labels.

Conclusions and Evaluation

Task 17 For each of the points below, **explain** why they are important for producing **accurate** and **reproducible** results.

> **Swirling** the conical flask whilst adding the hydrochloric acid.

> **Printing out** a black cross instead of drawing one.

Key Definitions
Accurate results
Results that are close to the true value.
Reproducible results
Results which are very similar when the experiment is repeated by someone else.

Task 18 You've now studied **two activities** investigating how **concentration** affects **rates of reactions**.

What does the graph you plotted in **Task 16** show you about the **relationship** between the independent and dependent variables in **Activity 2**?

....

....

Do your results from **Activity 2** line up with your results from **Activity 1**? Explain your answer.

....

....

Activity 1 involved **measuring gas production** using a measuring cylinder.
Activity 2 involved **timing** how long you could **see a black cross** through a solution.
Which of these methods of measurement is likely to be more **reproducible**? Explain your answer.

....

....

....

....

In **Activity 2**, the experiment was run **three times** and the **mean** time taken for the cross to disappear was calculated. Explain the impact this is likely to have had on the results.

....

....

Exam-Style Questions

Task 19 Try these **exam-style** questions.

1   Marble chips are mostly made of calcium carbonate. They react with dilute hydrochloric acid to produce calcium chloride, carbon dioxide gas and water. The equation for this reaction is:

$$CaCO_{3(s)} + 2HCl_{(aq)} \rightarrow CaCl_{2(aq)} + CO_{2(g)} + H_2O_{(l)}$$

1.1 A student investigates the rate of this reaction at two different temperatures.
The graph below shows the volume of carbon dioxide produced over time at 20 °C.

Sketch a curve on the graph for the results you would expect to see if the experiment was repeated at 25 °C.

[2]

1.2 Design an experiment to investigate the effect of surface area on the reaction between marble chips and hydrochloric acid.
Include details of the apparatus you would use and any measurements you would make.

....

....

....

....

....

....

....

....

....

[6]

[Total 8 marks]

Background Knowledge

Required
Practical 12

This practical is all about **paper chromatography**. There's a good chance you've come across it before — it's a handy technique that can be used to **separate** and **identify** the different substances in a mixture.

Task 1 Fill in the gaps in the table below to complete the terms and their definitions.

Term	Definition
Soluble	
	Will not dissolve.
	The liquid that something is dissolved in.
Solute	
Solution	

Task 2 In chromatography there is always a **stationary phase** and a **mobile phase**. Label the stationary phase and the mobile phase on the chromatography experiment shown below.

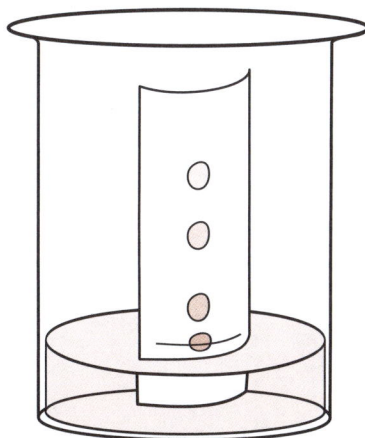

Key Definitions
Stationary Phase
In chromatography, a solid or really thick liquid where molecules are unable to move.

Mobile Phase
In chromatography, a gas or liquid where molecules are able to move.

Task 3 Explain, in terms of the stationary phase and mobile phase, why paper chromatography can be used to separate the substances in a mixture.

....

....

....

....

....

Practical

Task 4 Paper chromatography can be used to investigate the composition of a mixture of food colourings. The procedure for this experiment is shown below, but the steps have been mixed up. Put the steps in the correct order. The first one has been done for you.

1   *D*

2

3

4

5

6

A Mark how far up the paper the water travelled.

B Fill the bottom of the beaker to a depth of 1 cm with water, then place the bottom edge of the chromatography paper into the water.

C Wait until the water has nearly reached the top of the paper, then remove the paper from the beaker.

D Take a beaker and a piece of chromatography paper. Draw a line across the paper, approximately 2 cm from the bottom.

E Leave the paper to dry.

F At evenly spaced points along the line, place a spot of the unknown mixture and a spot of each of four known food colourings and label them.

Task 5 Look at step **D** in the method above.   What would you use to draw the line, and why? Are there any other steps in the method where you might need to make similar considerations?

What you'd use	Why

Other steps

Task 6 Explain a modification you should make to the method shown above if the solvent is volatile.

....

....

Key Definition
Volatile
Has a low boiling point.

DISCUSS # I'm in my stationery phase — I just love a good gel pen...
Not all mixtures can be separated by paper chromatography, sadly. Discuss with a partner what needs to happen in order for it to work, and suggest some reasons why a mixture might not be separated by it.

Results and Analysis

Task 7 Karim carried out the experiment using a mixture of food colourings, **M**, and known food colourings **W**, **X**, **Y** and **Z**. He obtained the chromatogram shown below.

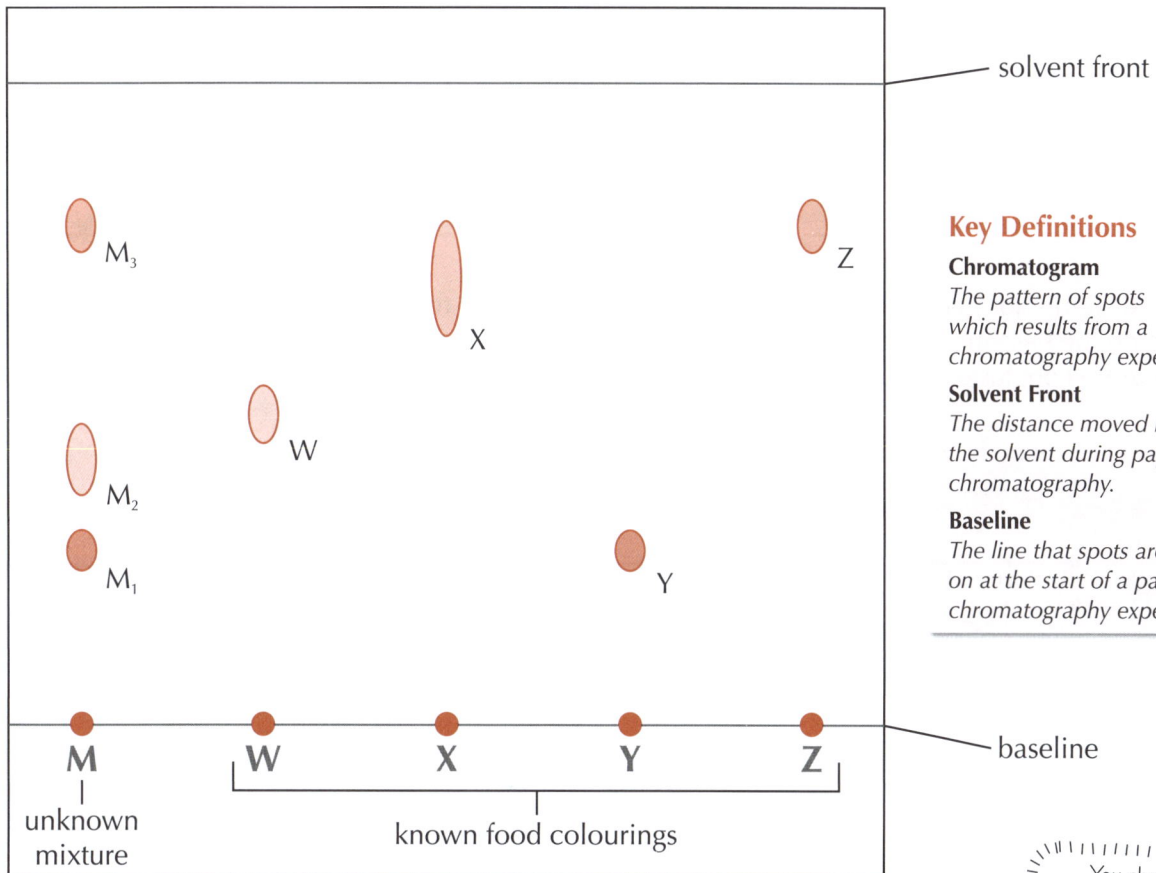

— solvent front

Key Definitions

Chromatogram
The pattern of spots which results from a chromatography experiment.

Solvent Front
The distance moved by the solvent during paper chromatography.

Baseline
The line that spots are placed on at the start of a paper chromatography experiment.

— baseline

M — unknown mixture

known food colourings

You should measure to the centre of each spot.

Starting from the baseline, measure the distance travelled by the solvent and each spot. Fill in your answers in the table below. Give your answers to 1 decimal place.

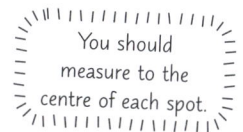

	Solvent	Spot M_1	Spot M_2	Spot M_3	Spot W	Spot X	Spot Y	Spot Z
Distance Travelled (cm)								

Task 8 An R_f value is a ratio that compares how far a substance travelled up a chromatogram compared to the solvent. It can be calculated using the equation:

$$R_f = \frac{\text{distance travelled by substance}}{\text{distance travelled by solvent}}$$

Use the equation to calculate the R_f value for each spot on the chromatogram. Give your answers to 2 significant figures.

	Spot M_1	Spot M_2	Spot M_3	Spot W	Spot X	Spot Y	Spot Z
R_f value							

Conclusions and Evaluation

Task 9 Which of food colourings **W**, **X**, **Y** or **Z**, could be present in mixture **M**?
Tick the boxes of any you think are present.

W ☐   X ☐

Y ☐   Z ☐

Explain your choice(s)

Task 10 Karim looks closely at his chromatogram and notices that some of mixture
M stayed on the baseline. Circle the correct options in the sentence below to give the
most accurate conclusion he can draw about the **number of substances** in mixture **M**.

There are   **exactly / at least / fewer than**   **two / three / four**   substances in mixture **M**.

Suggest why some of the mixture stayed on the baseline.

....

Task 11 Explain two reasons why it would be a good idea
for Karim to repeat the experiment using a **different solvent**.

1.

2.

Task 12 Karim wants to identify the substance that produced the spot M_2 on the chromatogram.

How could Karim modify his experiment to try and identify this substance?

....

....

Out damned spot! Out! Oh wait, that's a chromatogram...

DISCUSS

Why do you think it's important to remove the paper from the solvent before the solvent reaches the
top of the paper? Discuss with a partner. (Hint: think about what you need to calculate R_f values.)

Exam-Style Questions

Task 13 Try these **exam-style** questions.

1   A student is doing a paper chromatography experiment to investigate the composition of a sample of ink, **S**. The student runs the sample against some known dyes, **L**, **M** and **N**, in water and in ethanol. **Figure 1** shows the chromatogram produced in water.

1.1   In **Figure 1**, the R_f value for dye **N** is 0.48.
The water moved 12.5 cm.
Using the formula for R_f, calculate
the distance that dye **N** moved.

Figure 1

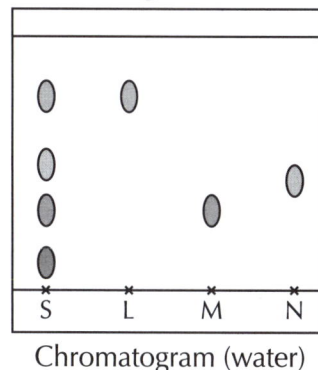

Chromatogram (water)

.... cm
[2]

1.2   Use **Figure 1** to explain which of dyes **L** and **N** will have the greater R_f value in water.

....

....
[1]

Table 1 shows the R_f values the student calculated for the same substances in ethanol.

Table 1

	S	L	M	N
R_f value(s) in ethanol	0.0, 0.27, 0.43, 0.73	0.21	0.43	1.1

1.3   The student's R_f value for dye **N** in **Table 1** is incorrect. How you can tell?

....
[1]

1.4   Use **Figure 1** and **Table 1** to explain which, if any, of dyes **L**, **M** and **N** could be in sample **S**.

....

....

....
[2]

1.5   Use **Table 1** to explain which of dyes **L** and **M** is more soluble in ethanol.

....

....

....
[3]

[Total 9 marks]

<table>
<tr><td>Required
Practical 13</td><td colspan="2"># Background Knowledge</td></tr>
</table>

Water purification might not be the most glamorous subject, but it's pretty useful.
Without **clean water**, we'd all be drinking nothing but fruit juice and bathing in milk like Cleopatra.

Task 1   **Litmus** and **universal indicator** are two examples of indicators.
Fill in the table below **comparing** these two indicators.
Give as much information as you can.

Key Definition
Indicator
A dye that changes colour depending on the pH.

	Litmus	Universal Indicator
Description of colour change		
What would you use it for?		
How is it used? E.g. solution, paper or both		

Task 2   Water from different **natural sources** can be treated to supply **potable water**. The main sources are **fresh water** and **sea water**. Complete the mind map below to **compare** these two sources of potable water.

Key Definition
Potable water
Water that is safe for humans to drink.

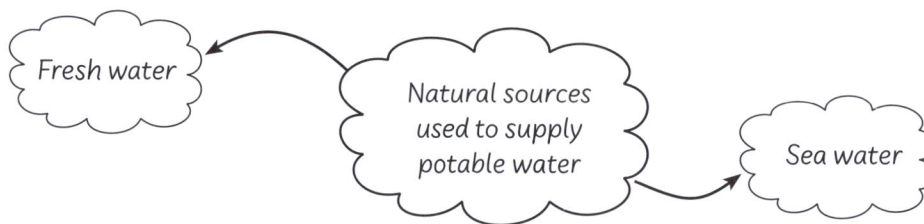

Fresh water ← Natural sources used to supply potable water → Sea water

Think about why each type of water needs treating, how it's treated and where the different supplies are used.

<table>
<tr><td>DISCUSS</td><td>## Indicators are just dyeing to tell you what the pH is...
With a partner, see if you can remember any other indicators you've used. How do they compare to litmus and universal indicator? What other ways are there to investigate the pH of a solution?</td></tr>
</table>

Practical — Activity 1

Task 3 In the box below, give a brief **outline** of how you could use the equipment shown to determine the **pH** of a series of **water samples**.

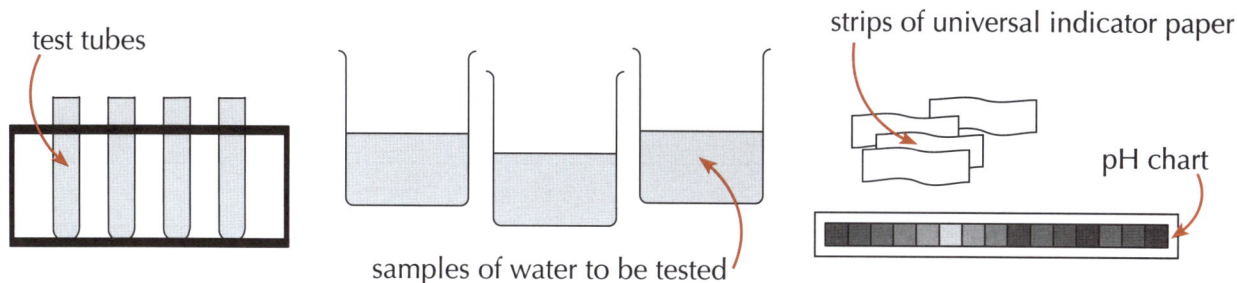

test tubes

strips of universal indicator paper

pH chart

samples of water to be tested

Task 4 This procedure can be used to find the mass of **dissolved solids** in a sample of water.

Procedure

1 Use a mass balance to accurately measure the mass of an evaporating basin.
   Record the mass of the empty basin.
2 Place the evaporating basin on a tripod and gauze over a Bunsen burner.
3 Pour a measured volume of the water sample into the basin.
4 Light the Bunsen burner and heat the evaporating basin until most of the water has evaporated.
5 Allow the basin to cool and the remaining water to evaporate.
   Crystals of any dissolved solids should be left behind in the basin.
6 Re-weigh the basin on the mass balance. Record the mass of the basin and its contents.

The **mass balance** used in this experiment should be able to measure a mass in grams to at least **two decimal places**. Suggest why this is important.

....

....

Sometimes, this method will give a value for the mass of dissolved solids that is **lower** than the **true mass**. Suggest one reason this might happen.

....

....

Analysis and Evaluation

Task 5   Give one **disadvantage** of using **universal indicator** to measure the pH of a water sample. Suggest what you could use **instead** that would address this disadvantage.

....

....

....

Task 6   Miles tested the **pH** of water samples from three **different sources**. His results are shown in the table.

Sample	A	B	C
pH	7	6	4

Miles wrote down two **conclusions**.
For each one, explain why Miles was **wrong** to make that conclusion from his results.

Sample A is neutral, so it must be pure water with no dissolved substances.

....

....

Sample C is more acidic than sample B, so C must have a greater mass of dissolved substances than B.

....

....

Task 7   Miles used **evaporation** to find the mass of dissolved solid in a 10 cm³ sample of water from **source C**. His results are shown in the table.

Evaporation of 10 cm³ sample from source C	
Mass of empty evaporating basin	22.46 g
Mass of basin after evaporating water sample	22.74 g

Calculate the **concentration** of dissolved solid in the water sample from source C in **g/dm³**.

Water source C is not necessarily "water, source: sea"

DISCUSS

You can't tell from these tests what substances are dissolved in a water sample.
Discuss with a partner what sort of tests might help to identify the dissolved substances.

Practical — Activity 2

Task 8 The apparatus shown in the diagram below can be used to **distil** a sample of water. Use the diagram to **complete the steps** of the procedure.

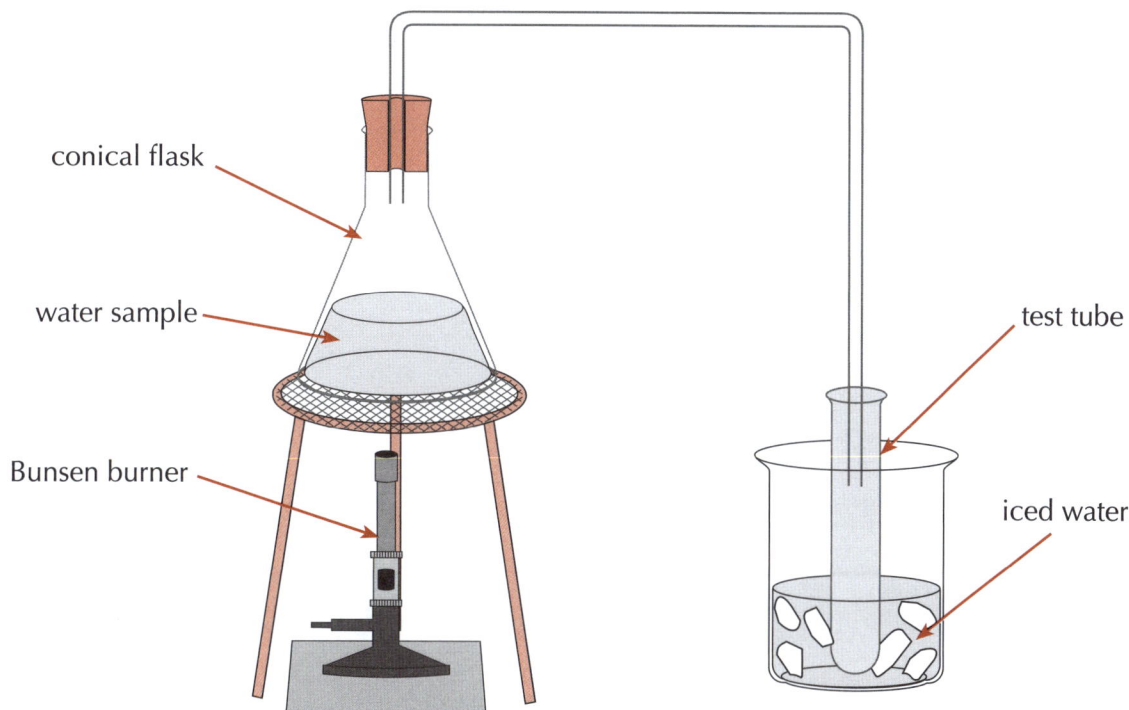

conical flask

water sample

Bunsen burner

test tube

iced water

Procedure

1 Stand an empty test tube _____ .

2 Put _____ in a conical flask,

and place this on a tripod and gauze over a Bunsen burner.

3 Connect the conical flask to _____

via glass or rubber tubing which passes through _____ .

4 Light the Bunsen burner and _____ .

The steam will pass through the tubing and condense _____ .

5 Continue gently _____ until you have 1-2 cm of water in the test tube.

6 Turn off the Bunsen burner. You will have _____ in the test tube.

Any _____ or insoluble impurities from

the original water sample will _____ .

Yes, those are supposed to be bits of ice, not crisps...

DISCUSS

The diagram above shows only the essential equipment to carry out the experiment. What other pieces of equipment might be useful to make this experiment go smoothly? Discuss with a partner.

Practical — Activity 2

Task 9 Instead of using the set-up shown in **Task 8**, you can also separate water from dissolved solids by simple distillation using a **condenser**. Draw and label a **diagram** showing the set-up for this method.

Include labels to show where the water goes in and out of the condenser.

Task 10 Water containing dissolved substances is a **mixture**.
Explain how you could use the different properties of pure substances and mixtures to **confirm** that the product of a distillation experiment is **pure water**.

....
....
....
....
....
....
....
....

Key Definitions

Mixture
Two or more substances that are combined, but not chemically bonded.

Pure substance
A substance containing only one element or compound.

Results, Analysis and Evaluation

Task 11 **Evaporation** and **distillation** can both be used to separate dissolved solids from liquids.
Suggest why distillation has been used instead of evaporation in this part of this practical.

....

....

....

Task 12 A student is given instructions for the
procedure shown in **Task 8**. The instructions contain the
following **warnings**. For each one, say why you think it
would cause a problem if the advice is not followed.

Hint: Both these warnings are to stop the water ending
up in the wrong place. What would happen if it did?

When heating the conical flask, do not
allow the water to boil too vigorously
and reach the top of the flask.

Make sure the end of the tube leading
into the test tube always remains
well above the level of the distilled
water that has been collected.

Task 13 Look back at **Task 6** and **Task 7**. Miles continued his investigation of his water samples.
He distilled a sample of water from source C. He then **repeated** his tests from Tasks 6 and 7
on samples of the distilled water he collected. Explain how this will help Miles **confirm**
that he carried out the distillation correctly, and what **results** he should expect.

....

....

....

De-still-ation is how they make sparkling water...

DISCUSS

Compare the distillation apparatus used in Task 8 with the diagram you drew in Task 9. Discuss with a
partner the advantages and disadvantages of each method. Which would you use, and why?

Exam-Style Questions

Task 14 Try these **exam-style** questions.

1   A student is investigating the water quality of a local river. The student collects a number of water samples from a part of the river near their home over the course of one afternoon.

1.1   Suggest two ways the student could improve this sampling to be more representative.

1 ....

....

2 ....

....

[2]

1.2   The student tests a sample of pure water alongside the samples from the river.
Suggest why the student does this.

....

....

....

[1]

1.3   The student discovers that their supply of pure water has been contaminated with an impurity.
The student believes that this impurity is sodium chloride. Describe how the student could:
- obtain a solid sample of the dissolved impurity,
- measure the mass of the sample of the impurity obtained, and
- carry out tests to confirm the water contains sodium chloride.

....

....

....

....

....

....

....

....

....

....

....

[6]

[Total 9 marks]

CGP

Chemistry Required Practicals? CGP has the solution!

Ace the practical questions for GCSE AQA Combined Science Higher...

- **Tasks to boost your background knowledge...**
  So you can put your scientific thinking to the test

- **Activities on results, analysis and evaluation...**
  Yep — we've got every Required Practical covered

- **Exam-style questions for extra practice...**
  Of course — these will get you ready for the real thing!

- **Plus online sample answers for the whole book...**
  Perfect for seeing what you're aiming for!

Practical makes perfect... or practice makes practical... you know what I mean! ☺

P.S. Don't miss our Required Practicals Course Booklets for GCSE AQA Biology and Physics!

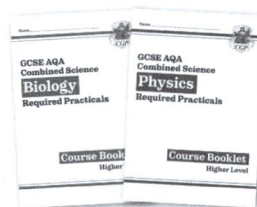

GCSE AQA Combined Science **Biology** Required Practicals — **Course Booklet** Higher

GCSE AQA Combined Science **Physics** Required Practicals — **Course Booklet** Higher Level

Press here for nightvision mode

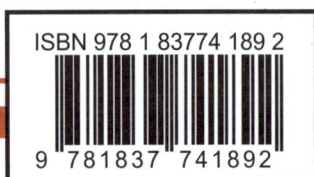

ISBN 978 1 83774 189 2

9 781837 741892

SCCAHPL41

CGP — books like no others!

Scan here for retail price

www.cgpbooks.co.uk